The Garage Sale Book

The

Garage Sale

Book

Turn Your Trash Into Cash

Jeff Groberman and Colin Yardley

 Prima Publishing & Communications
Post Office Box 1260GY
Rocklin, CA 95677
Telephone: (916) 624-5718

Cover Design: Hatley Mason

Prima Publishing & Communications
P.O. Box 1260GY
Rocklin, CA 95677
(916) 624-5718

Library of Congress Cataloging-in-Publication Data

Groberman, Jeff.
   The garage sale book.

   1. Garage sales. I. Yardley, Colin.
II. Title.
HF5482.3.G76 1987   658.8'7   86-25388
ISBN 0-914629-10-7

10   9   8   7   6   5   4   3   2   1

Printed in the United States of America

"It's not junk until it's been in three garage sales."

Doc Harris

Contents

Acknowledgments

The authors wish to express their gratitude to Michele Groberman, whose ingenuity provided the signs, maps, and suggested layouts for this book. We wish to further thank family and friends who supported this enterprise both financially and through their strong moral support.

A Few Words to Our Readers

We have spent many enjoyable hours researching this book. Let's face it, we *do* like to sniff through other people's belongings, and we're not going to stay in the closet about it any longer! While pursuing our passion, we have purchased an unbelievable amount of junk, which we've had to unload at our own garage sales.

This book is chock-full of sage advice to help not only the garage-sale rookie but also the experienced back-yard entrepreneur.

Garage sales are a relatively new phenomenon (there is no mention of them in Homer or Euclid and only a passing reference in Milton), so there's still a lot to lawn....er, learn.

Enjoy! But most of all, get rid of that junk!

CHAPTER 1

Why Have a Garage Sale?

Congratulations! You have just bought the first item for your garage sale: this book! (We'll bet this modest little volume is one of your first sales.)

Who has garage sales? Everyone! They're one of society's great equalizers. Socialites have garage sales in Beverly Hills where they're called "yard sales, dahlings." They have them in Detroit: "Hey, Man, wanna buy some hubcaps? How 'bout the whole car?" It's even rumored that the Queen of England had a garage sale — sold off some hardly used "possessions" and some family jewels — much to Philip's chagrin.

Why Have a Garage Sale?

Why have a garage sale? Most likely, it's to get rid of all that junk that's been slowly filling up the attic, the basement, and the crawl spaces — all those things that have been squeezing you and the kids out toward the sidewalk. Then there's all the priceless pack-rat treasure you stored at your mother's, aunt's, or good friend's when you hauled yourself off to college. It's all stuff that good garage sales are made of. Fact is, people will buy *anything*! It doesn't matter how broken, beat-up, offbeat, or off-the-wall it is. If the price is right there's a buyer for it somewhere. Remember pet rocks, canned air, and Ford Pintos?

But there's also another good reason for throwing a garage sale. You can make money! How much money? Well, that really depends on you. It can be as little as a hundred dollars or a whole lot more. Most people drastically underestimate what they will make and are very surprised when they add up the day's sales.

Having a garage sale can also be fun! You get a chance to meet a lot of people you've never talked to before, like the next-door neighbors and such. Given the invitation, few can resist the urge to rummage through other people's junk.

A good garage sale can take on the festive air of a community bazaar. Total strangers who wouldn't give you the time of day on the street are suddenly friendly and even chummy. Most want to offer advice or tell you that they have junk "just like yours." Yes, you can meet a lot of interesting people during the snoop and haggle of a garage sale.

If you're terrifically ambitious, you might even make the event a neighborhood garage sale and attract buyers from the adjoining neighborhood. (More on this later.)

Throwing a successful garage sale — one that is both fun and profitable — is a bit of an art. With some effort and a little planning, it will definitely pay off.

CHAPTER 2

When?

When to have a garage sale? In the *Rig Veda* , the ancient Hindu account of creation, there are listed no less than twenty-eight auspicious days each year on which to "barter old baggage." The Tibetan *Book of the Boulders* cautions against holding garage sales during any period when the goddess Kingvat is "unloading on the mountain people."

LET'S SET UP THE FRAGILE STUFF TOMORROW.

When?

Astrologers and bio-rhythm experts have their own theories. There is even the neo-Pythagorean dictum that a garage sale held during any calendar day which is a prime number of the tetractys will meet with only limited success.

We have generally found that weekends are good.

The question is whether to hold it over two days or to do the whole shebang in one — and if so, which one?

If you have the time and the patience, obviously two days are better. If you do decide to turn your garage sale into a two-day festival, remember to add enough time to set everything up and tear everything down. You won't necessarily get double the crowd but you will probably get a significant increase over one day. In addition, you stand a better chance if you get rained out one of the days.

There's a lot of discussion on which day is the better one. You've probably heard some of it yourself at the bingo table or in the beauty salon. Some people claim that Saturday is better because more people are out buying things on a Saturday. Others claim Sunday because a lot of people are out and not as many stores are open, hence less competition.

Frankly, we have found that it doesn't make a lot of difference, and when you get right down to it, the Tibetan system is probably as good as any other. There is no rational pattern to *when* or *why* people will buy things…
… but you certainly can hedge your bets if you follow some of the suggestions in this book.

"What about long weekends?" we hear some of you cry. We generally try to avoid them. We find that a lot of people make plans on long weekends — plans to be out of town — and you often don't draw as big a crowd.

The time of year can also make a difference. Traditionally (that is, since 1901 when Abner Skeat invented the garage), we have found that the biggest crowds always seem to emerge in late May and June. If you live in the sun belt where it's late May and June nine months of the year, then it doesn't really matter much. However, up in the often-intemperate temperate zone, we find that by the late-May thaw most folks are tired of being cooped up all winter and are out and about cruising in their cars looking for something meaningful to do (or to buy). Something about wet or snowy days isn't conducive to bargain hunting. The next best time for your sale is in late summer

— just before school starts. People seem to have a lot of sales then and try to unload last year's junk.

Of course, you can have a garage sale anytime ....

HONEST BOB'S
FABULOUS GIGANTIC
PRE-CHRISTMAS
GARAGE SALE

... but, on the whole, if you have a choice, you should look for dates in late spring or late summer.

You should also give some thought as to the actual *time* you would like your garage sale to begin. Traditionally, most begin at nine or ten in the morning and run until mid-afternoon. However, because garage sales are becoming more and more of a national pastime, the competition for customers is becoming more and more fierce. Therefore, you may want to start yours earlier.

Did you know that many Garage Sale Cruisers (GSCs) actually sit up the night before with the classifieds and a road map and plan out a route to hit the most garage sales in one day? Strange but true! So if you started your garage sale at 8:00 AM, you would probably snag a lot of these people because they could hit your place first! Of course, the Early Birds, the strangest of all scavengers, would be out even earlier! But more on this in another chapter.

We have also found that most garage sales do their highest volume of business in the first few hours. So staying open late will probably not be worth it. Generally by about 3:30 PM most people are "garaged out."

CHAPTER 3

Scout the Territory

Okay, now that you've bought this book.... or are you still browsing through it, waiting for the store clerk to scowl at you over his horn rims? If that's the case, close it up, take it to the cash register and buy it NOW! Remember, you can sell it again, so it hardly costs anything! And hey, don't be offended by the hard sell. It's hard sell that's made this country what it is today.... *Fantasy Island* for the criminally indisposed.

The first thing you want to do is spend a couple of weekends scouting *other people's* garage sales.

This means you must work at refining your perceptions until you actually start to notice all those homemade **GARAGE SALE** signs stuck on telephone poles around your neighborhood....

You might want to stop at the odd garage sale on your way to the corner store or the quilting bee. This will serve as a good introduction to garage sales in general and, as an added bonus, you may find bargains you will scarcely believe. For example, we found a fantastic seaworthy skiff for use at our oceanside summer cabin and paid a whopping twenty bucks! Several garage sales later we saw other skiffs similar to our little beauty for which the asking price was several hundred dollars. We also picked up a sixty-dollar boat ladder for two dollars and, eh, well, we....er....we also bought a lot of junk. But what the heck, we sold it at *our* garage sales.

So take a look at what your neighbors are doing and don't be afraid to tell them you are planning your own garage sale. Everyone has advice, and most love to dispense it. Also check out the layout of each garage sale. You'll begin to notice some basic indicators which spell the difference between a rousing success and a so-so occasion. Does the sale look grungy? By this, we mean do you feel the urge to wash your hands just looking at the stuff? Is it neatly laid out or do you have to dig to find things? Are the prices marked? Are items dusty or polished?

You will quickly develop an appreciation for the people who have spent a little time and effort on their sale. The merchandise looks inviting and, of course, such sales inevitably seem to attract a whole bunch of people. Check out the prices for various items and watch what sells. You'll get a good idea of what to ask for your own stuff.

One word of warning. If you take kids, watch out! Other kids' toys, no matter how broken, mangled, scabious, or thrashed are always irresistible and simply must be had! You can have some horrible scenes.

What we suggest is either giving them a couple of dollars or limiting them to a certain portion of their allowance with which to purchase a dog-chewed *Master of the Universe* or a one-eyed dolly. You'll find they will then be easier to handle — and a buck or two for a whole day's peace and quiet, *plus* their learning a few fundamentals on being a consumer, will be well worth it.

CHAPTER 4

It's a Lovely Day in the Neighborhood

As soon as the word get's out that you're having a garage sale you'll start to get requests from friends, relatives, and neighbors like:

And of course you don't want to say no. But be careful or before you know it, Grandma Ethel's stack of *National Enquirers* and Uncle Ernie's badly stained mattress may make your neighbors wonder what kind of cat you really are.

Not to worry. You can preview items *before* they are brought over to your place and diplomatically indicate which ones you will take and which ones you won't.

In many cases, friends and relatives will offer to help out. This can be a golden opportunity to increase the scope of your garage sale. And remember, the bigger the sale the better. *But* , as it grows in size, the more help you're going to need. So, if people have more than an item or two, suggest that they join you and make it a two- or three-family garage sale. People like to visit multiple garage sales because these greatly increase the chances of finding fabled bargains without having to hunt and travel all over. The best plan of all is to go all out and make it a neighborhood garage sale.

Properly promote a multiple garage sale and you will be amazed at the response. We have attended several of these which have drawn enormous crowds and have taken on an almost carnival-like atmosphere. In marketing terms, we are talking the basic "shopping mall" concept: One store will attract only so many people, while several stores will attract shoppers from far and wide. In addition to the sophisticated economics of a neighborhood-wide sale, there are some social benefits. You'll reacquaint yourself with old neighbors as well as meet some new ones. Generally, these events usually wrap up with a neighborhood pot luck dinner or barbecue, a "Greek Day" dance in the streets, a fireworks display, and two or three unexpected births.

There are essentially two sure-fire ways of throwing such an extravaganza:

1. Everyone displaying at their own garage
2. Everyone at one location

Much depends upon the number of families involved. Sometimes these things can spread like wildfire and stretch over several square blocks, leading to intermarriage and other complications.

If one person has a big backyard or if the neighborhood has a vacant lot, the space can be filled with a number of "booths." Each booth can represent a family or each can be allocated for a special department such as "books," "toys," "housewares," "hardware," and the like. The method of keeping track of who makes how much will be discussed in the chapter on prices.

It really isn't that hard to organize a neighborhood garage meet. What it requires is one person to start the ball rolling, and since you bought the book, guess who's elected.

The first thing to do is to contact your neighbors. If you're confident, outgoing, and garrulous, you can just phone 'em right up or pitch the idea across the back fence. If you're a tad more introverted (that is, you wear your underwear inside your clothes), you can make a little flyer like the one shown on page 29 and put it in everyone's mail box. When people respond, set up a neighborhood meeting some evening a month or so in advance to lay out the ground rules and assignments.

Some of the choices and assignments you must make:

- dates(s)
- time
- separate locations or one central sale?
- pricing (see chapter on pricing)
- Will it be a department store set-up?
- food and refreshments
- share advertising costs and work on signs
- schedule for cash desk
- cleanup

Howdy Neighbor

We're planning to get rid of our "old jun
and excess heirlooms" and make mone
too.
    We're planning a Garage Sale!
Why don't you join us? After all

    The Bigger the Better
    The More the Merrier
Why not have a neighborhood garage
sale and party?
If you've got a basement, attic, craw
space full of stuff and you're
interested in making this a
    Neighborhood Event
please come to a meeting
    Wednesday April 3rd at 7:30pm
Are you interested but can't attend
the meeting, please phone

                    Joe and Barb Jones
                    1213 Dogwood
                    263 4985

Once you have somebody in charge and everyone's tasks allocated, the sale should run itself. In fact, we have found that most neighborhoods that have held a collective garage sale will generally repeat it every year as a neighborhood event. It seems like a socially acceptable way for people to meet neighbors who have lived next to each other for years but who have never really met. And, of course, it can be profitable. Very profitable! In fact, we might even go so far as to say that a good, rip-roaring profitable neighborhood garage sale is a darn good form of group therapy.... but we won't go that far.

One word of caution: In eyeing your neighbors' displays, be careful not to end up with more junk than you started with.

CHAPTER 5

Kids Are Entrepreneurs, Too

Garage sales are a terrific way to entertain the kids and teach them some basic marketplace smarts. Don't be surprised if they catch on real fast and outsell you.

(Remember the first time you took the little novice fishing and the trout lined up for a chance at *his* hook?) Here are a few basics for harmonious family involvement.

Once you announce that you're having a garage sale, the kids will most assuredly want to get in on it. And don't expect the little darlings to cling tearfully to their old toys. We've found that, quite to the contrary, they generally want to sell everything! The possibility that they can make **MONEY** to buy *more* junk positively inspires the wee capitalists. This can create problems. There are certain gifts that you won't want them to part with. Try to pre-screen their toys one night when they're asleep and convince them that this is the pile they want to sell. You

will probably have to bargain over a few pieces, but generally this works. Also, you will have to go over all their pricing; otherwise, you might find them selling that two-hundred-dollar Swahili-speaking pet robot for twenty-five cents.

There is also the issue of what happens to the proceeds of the kids' sales. Some kids, believe it or not, will argue that every cent from the sale of their toys belongs to them. It doesn't matter that *you* bought the toys. They claim the toys are theirs, and, if necessary, they'll get Forensics to show you *their* fingerprints all over each one. Here are some compromises:

1. We split the proceeds because *we* , good old Mommy and Daddy, will be buying them their new toys.... right?

2. The money goes directly into their bank account.

3. The money is earmarked for *them* to buy gifts for other people at Christmas and for birthdays.... "The last time we just *gave* you five dollars, you came home with an eight-pound bag of ju jubes, and we can't have that again, can we, dear?" They'll understand.

4. They are allowed to keep a percentage of the toy take and the rest goes into their bank account.

Let them get involved in making the signs and in other aspects of the sale. Set them up with their own table, but make sure that *you* handle the cash. Tell them they will get *theirs* at the end when you tally up accounts. This keeps some control on what they are actually selling their stuff for and ensures that no money gets lost.

If the toys have been taken care of, properly maintained, and fairly priced, they'll sell a lot of them to all the neighbor kids as well as to any kids that might stop by. The economies of many struggling nations would boom overnight if they sold toys (a gem of economic wisdom offered free with the price of this book), so don't be surprised if the kids make a *lot* of money. Step in, however, if you see them auctioning off baby brother.

CHAPTER 6

Advertise

You can have the world's greatest garage sale with the best bargains, but it won't matter a darn if people don't know about it.

It never ceases to amaze us that people will go to a lot of effort to mount a garage sale, then stick up one little hand-scrawled sign and wonder why nobody shows up. With a little inventive advertising, you can have a crowd of people beating a path to your garage or front lawn.

The first place to begin is the newspapers. Most daily and weekly community newspapers have a classified section and even a separate listing for garage sales where they offer space for specially reduced fees. With their large circulation, they are, by far, the best place to advertise. There are also the "buy and sell" type of neighborhood tabloids that carry advertising free of charge or for a very small fee. For best results, put the announcement of your garage sale in as many of these as possible. Remember that most of them require at least a week's notice.

GARAGE SALE
Sat Nov 2, 11am-4pm.
2329 Huron Drive Coquitlam

Moving Overseas - Misc
household, tools, etc.
115-6655 Lynas Lane Rmd

Household moving sale,
6 years worth of
gathered possessions.
A few antiques and
collectibles, 6 piece
serving Royal Albert china
colour tv, stereo,
everything from plants to
furniture and in between
babys cribs and clothes,
will sell as package,
make the best deal of
your life! 143 West 48th
Ave or call 327-5587

O NO INDICATION AS TO what sort of stuff is available!

Basement & Garage Sales

MOVING SALE
Contemporary furnishings.
Some Danish teak. Large
Batiks from Bali. Lots of
bargains. By appointment
only. 273-4200 after 5pm.

Moving sale, samples, wall
paper, magazines, pictures,
frames, accessories,
household items, clothes,
toys, plant lights,
lawnmower, tools. 822
Rodchester Ave. Coquitlam
Nov. 2nd & 3rd, 10am-4pm

⌐ BOUND TO get huge crowd!

✓ good, ✓ but they'll ✓ have ✓ early birds

Quality 2 family garage
sale, 5331 Woodpecker Drive
5320 Woodpecker Drive,
Richmond, Sat Oct 26th 10-4

Moving sale, samples, wall
paper, magazines, pictures,
frames, accessories,
household items, clothes,
toys, plant lights,
lawnmower, tools. 822
Rodchester Ave. Coquitlam
Nov. 2nd & 3rd, 10am-4pm

VANCOUVER Mega Garage Sale, Sat Nov 2, 9am
4147 YUCULTA CRESCENT (in Salish Park).
VANCOUVER: Garage Moving Sale, Sat & Sun, Nov
2-3. 3687 BLENHEIM STREET.
VANCOUVER Multi Family Sale, Sat Nov 2
10am-3pm. 2395 WEST 7TH AVENUE (corner of 7th
& Balsam).
VANCOUVER: 4 Family Basement Sale, Sat Nov 2
11am-4pm (no early birds). 884 EAST 53RD AVENUE
VANCOUVER: Garage Sale, Nov 2, 10am-2pm. 2615
EAST 53 AVENUE.
VANCOUVER: Giant Moving Sale, Sat & Sun Nov
2-3, 10am-4pm. 1156 CONNAUGHT DRIVE (betw
Oak & Granville).

This one costs, so keep it brief.

Same ad in free paper. Make it large.

Garage Sales	121

Mega Garage Sale

Sat. Nov. 2nd, **4147
Yuculta Cres.** Vancouver
(Salish Park west Ker-
risdale) 9 a.m. No early
birds.

Sat. Nov. 2 , proceeds to
go to Single Moms Support
Group. Rosewood Rec
Hall, **8280 No. 2 Rd.**

What should the ad say? First, it must contain the vital information and second, it should pique interest. Make sure the ad contains the following:

When: The date(s) and time. If you aren't specific about the time, you might find yourself hounded by Early Birds. We have more on how to deal with these dreaded pests later.

Where: Give the address, of course, but if you live in an area that might be difficult to find, give a hint: "just off Elm Street" or "near Granville and 70th."

What: If you have a lot of something or something special or out of the ordinary, like children's clothes or records or electronics, by all means, say so. Many collectors look for specific categories when scanning the garage-sale section of the paper.

Conditions: Say whether your garage sale will be canceled in the event of poor weather.

Promote: If it is a multi-family garage sale, say so. If it's your first garage sale, say that, also. It will make your merchandise appear fresh (if that's possible for used items).

CHAPTER 7

Let the Signs Point the Way

One of the most effective ways of advertising is the use of signs. You probably have seen lots of them. Some are good, but most aren't. Generally, the simpler the sign the better. But first things first.

Signs have two functions. First, they advertise your garage sale and then they guide people to you. If you are lucky enough to live on a main thoroughfare, then you can get by with a lot fewer signs than if you live deep in the "sac end" of some obscure cul-de-sac.

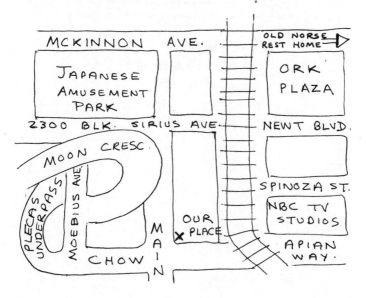

Signs that advertise should be large and flashy. You have a fair bit of information to get across, and if it is on an 8½" x 11" sheet of paper, nobody is going to notice it, let alone read it. Think big! You don't need a lot of signs, but they should be put up a day or so in advance in areas that get a heavy volume of traffic. They should be colorful and highlight the date(s) and address. You can make the signs on cardboard or on sheets of brown paper and then staple them to the backs of opened cardboard boxes for support. Unless you are absolutely convinced it won't rain, we'd suggest covering them with plastic wrap.

Gigantic
Garage Sale

1213 Dogwood

Sat. <u>and</u> Sun.
May 16 - 17
10 A.M - 3 P.M.

Something for
Everyone

Rain or Shine

Gigantic Garage Sale
1213 Dogwood
10 - 3

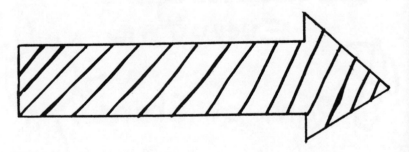

When you are affixing these signs to street posts and telephone poles, keep in mind that there may be by-laws prohibiting the posting of signs. We know everyone does it, but that's no excuse if you are that one unlucky person who's nailed while you're nailing your sign. We checked with several municipalities and found that they all had by-laws against it, but none of them enforce their laws if people use common sense and remove their signs when they are finished.

We have recently seen some new and very innovative signs. One woman with a lot of clothes and costumes to sell made up scarecrow-type signs — you know, two pieces of wood with a dress draped over them and a hat on top. She then stapled the garage sale sign to the "arm." It attracted a lot of attention — as well as two nearsighted neighbors who tried to date "them."

With the onset of computer sign-making programs we're beginning to see more and more computer-generated signs. Ah, progress!

Some people make a sandwich board and place it on their car roof. They then park the car at a strategic point. You might consider this as an alternative if you can't use the utility poles or if you require someone's permission to put up a sign on the boulevard. If your eldest son belongs to the Steve Martin School of Public Exhibitionism, we suggest slapping an advertising sandwich board on him and letting him dance along beside the traffic. This is bound to do wonders for attracting attention to your sale, not to mention what it will do for the property values in your neighborhood.

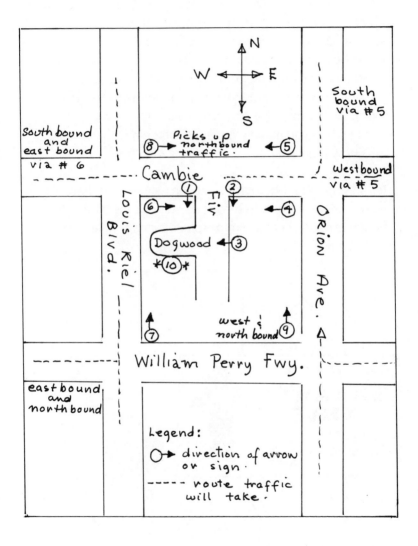

A second set of signs should go up early on the morning of sale day. These can be smaller and should simply spell out the words "Garage Sale," your address, and an arrow pointing in the direction. You should put one of these signs up at every point where a person must make a turn. Don't be afraid to make a lot of these signs. Remember, people will be coming from *both* directions on each possible route, so plan these out on the map and number them. Also, remember to think which way drivers are facing when you make your signs, otherwise, half your arrows will be pointing in the wrong direction.

It's an unpleasant thought, but even as you read these words, there are hundreds of cars still circling aimlessly in neighborhoods because of misplaced garage-sale arrows.

Sign-making can be tedious, so try to split up the assignments and start early; otherwise, you might be up quite late making signs the night before the sale. One suggestion: Make a stencil and spray out your signs "el rapidemento." Remember, neatness counts. People will begin to form an opinion of your garage sale and whether or not they want to go to it when they see your sign. If it is hastily sprayed or sloppy they might feel inclined to believe that your goods will look the same. It's amazing, but people who are total slobs themselves and who dwell happily in abject pig-sty surroundings every day of their lives will judge your garage sale by the neatness of your sign. This is one of the deeper mysteries of the human situation and quite beyond the scope of this little volume.

Tip # 47:
USE THE GARAGE SALE TO GET TO KNOW YOUR NEIGHBORS.

WE HAVE A GREAT RELATIONSHIP. HENRY'S BOW LEGGED AND I PLAY CROQUET.

Also, don't forget to put a few handbills up in neighborhood laundromats, supermarkets, and community centers.

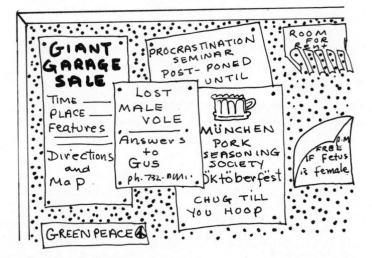

Finally, don't forget to take down all your signs when the garage sale is over; otherwise, you may continue to get visitors when you don't want them. It is just common decency to remove your signs after it's over because if you don't, you run the risk of having your neighbors refer to you as uncommonly indecent. Some of us care about what our neighbors think. Some of us care about animal husbandry and endocrinology, but let's not digress.

We've found that numbering each sign on a city street map is an invaluable aid when it comes time to locating each for removal. When possible, we've tried to recover them in as good a condition as possible so they might be used again (with the minor modification of the date).

CHAPTER 8

It's Raining!

Okay! You've done everything! You've priced all items, made the signs, placed the signs, gotten everything planned to a tee, and the forecast is for.... rain! As Karl Malden says, "What will you do? What will you do?"

Well, with a little extra planning you could have a contingency plan.

It's Raining!

When it comes down to it, you really only have two choices. You go ahead and have your sale, or you don't. The first thing you should do is decide whether or not you will go ahead in the event of rain. If you have no garage (i.e., it was going to be a *yard* sale), you should make sure your signs and ads say "Canceled if Rain" or "Wet Books for Sale" or something equally appropriate.

There is no doubt that rain *will* cut down on the attendance. However, you may be locked into the sale date for a variety of reasons, or you might even say, "What the heck, we'll have it anyway and then have another on a sunny day later on to get rid of what's left." (Some families actually reason like this.) If this is the case, you may increase your attendance by marking your ads and signs: **Rain or Shine.**

It's Raining!

If you do go ahead when it's raining, make sure you have everything under cover, but still make it evident that you *are, indeed,* having a garage sale.

Once again, with a little planning you can't go too far wrong.

★ ★ ★

"In Leningrad, in the 19th century, there are not very many garages."

Dostoevsky, *The Idiot*

CHAPTER 9

The Price Is Right

The big question is: What to charge?

Well, perhaps an equally big question is: How much of this junk do I *really* want to schlep back into the house, garage, attic, or crawl space? If the answer is none of it, then price it all **cheap** . We mean really cheap — under five dollars if it was originally a higher ticket item and under a dollar if you really want it to move.

Remember, people are looking for "bargoons."* If they want to spend the big bucks they'll go to Macy's. On the other hand, you may have certain things that you're reluctant to part with below a certain price. Ascertain that magic number and *stick to it!* If you're willing to flex a few bucks either way, please read the chapter on "The Art of Haggling."

If you're more interested in getting the top buck for certain items, you would be better off pursuing other alternatives for these items. For instance:

● Antiques – Take the stuff to a dealer and get a quote. You might be pleasantly surprised. On the other hand, you might be disappointed to find out that Aunt Matilda's da Vinci was signed with a ball point pen. Either way, you can always try to do better at the sale and use the dealer's price as a fallback.

TiP # 42: KNOW YOUR MARKET.

YOU MEATHEAD, THIS IS VINTAGE PLOTINUS! HOW DARE YOU OFFER ME A LOUSY 50 CENTS!

---

* bargoon: 1. a bastardization of "bargain" which is employed by seasoned auctioneers   2. an annoying person who inhabits taverns and lounges

- Collectibles – A friend of ours came across his old collection of baseball cards in the basement of his mother's house. He was going to pitch them in the garbage when he remembered reading an article which stated that certain cards were valuable. Acting on a hunch, he checked it out and found a book on the subject. Sure enough, he had some of the valuable cards. He nearly threw six thousand dollars in the trash. The same can hold true with comics and certain other memorabilia that people find valuable. If you think there might be even the slightest chance, check it out first. One man's worthless junk is another man's gold mine, and who are we to judge which of them is the nutbar?

Okay, in order that, under the guise of being informative, we don't completely avoid the issue of what to charge, here is a very rough rule of thumb:

Records: Fifty cents to a dollar for the oldies but goodies. More for recent but goodies. More still for real old oldies but goodies in real goodie shape.

Books: Paperbacks anywhere from ten cents to twenty-five cents. Even less if they're in sad shape. You also might move more of them if you make a volume offer, say four or five for a dollar. Hardcover books can go for a bit more, but I wouldn't get into anything over a couple of dollars unless it's a collector's item.

Household and bric-a-bracs: Try to keep all these items at under a dollar if possible.

Appliances and electronics: The best bet is to check out in the newspaper or your local "buy and sell" what they're going for and price them for less. Generally a half to a third the retail value if they are relatively current goods. If the stuff is old, like old tube radios, they might have to go for a lot less (unless you can pawn it off as a "future antique").

Most important, keep the prices low, otherwise a garage sale can be like a Thanksgiving dinner — you'll be dealing with leftovers for a long time.

CHAPTER 10

The Layout
(Yes, Neatness Counts)

First appearances count. People often cruise by and make a snap judgment on whether to stop or just keep going. If your garage sale looks like a laundromat hit by Libyan mortar shells, people are likely to keep on driving by.... except for the kind of people you probably wouldn't want around your children anyway.

Remember that you have to display your goods in an enticing way — something that advertisers and campaigning politicians have known from day one. Some suggestions:

1. Wash and iron all clothing. If it's clean enough to fool someone with 20-40 vision, just iron it. Place all pieces on hangers and mark the sizes plainly so that they can be seen. If your garments look neat and clean, you have a better chance of selling them.

2. Make sure that toys are complete and have all their parts. A He-Man with one leg is not a big seller.

3. Have enough table space. Nothing is worse than having to rummage through a lot of boxes, not knowing whether an old sneaker or a knife blade lies buried in the depths. Display your stuff in a neat, organized way. Anything that looks cared for looks more expensive.

4. If you have the original boxes in which things came, place the goods in them. Make sure all instruction manuals and applicable warranties are with each item. This shows that you are a caring, responsible person whose objects are probably in good shape.

5. Label and price everything legibly. Set up tables in categories, i.e.: "Housewares," "Hardware," "Electronic," "Toys," "Garden," and so on. If the item is obscure (Hungarian astrolabe, Yak nasal tweezers), place a card next to it that explains what it is. You might find someone buying it for Uncle Ernie who's been looking for one of those doohickies for a long time.

Remember, a little neatness and organization will snag a lot of casual passersby and will give them a chance to see all your wares. The last thing you want to hear a week later is: "Oh, did you have one of *those* ? If I had seen it I would have bought it." Make your category signs large and hang 'em high so people can see from the street that there may be something for them. Put all your best merchandise out front and mix and match categories enough to give passersby the impression there's something for everyone at your garage sale.

CHAPTER 11

Keeping Accounts

Keeping accounts is relatively important, particularly if it's a multi-family sale or if people in the family are expecting to see a return on *their* items. You don't want to hear yourself saying, "Our marriage broke up, your Honor, because he sold my Bobby Vinton records at our garage sale and kept the money." Marriages, as we all know, have ruptured for far less. With a little bit of planning, you can save a whole lot of hassle later.

The best way to do this is to keep an inventory. Make a list of every single item. In the first column next to each one mark down the asking price, and then enter beside that the actual sale price. That way you will know exactly what sold and for how much.

Another variation is to put a number on every price tag that corresponds to the number on the inventory list. In this way you don't have to keep looking up and down the list (or pages of lists) to locate the item. You just find the number on the list that corresponds to the number on the item and.... bingo!

A simple method that is useful in multi-family garage sales is to have a different color label for each family group and a matching color-coded cash box at the cash desk. If it's a "red" item, the money is deposited in the "red" cash box, etc. Keep an eye peeled for relatives who claim to be color blind. You'll have to be careful that you keep track of the accounts or you may be seeing "red" through "black" eyes.... nyuk, nyuk, nyuk.

You will also find it useful to have a "float" of some sort for making change. A float of about fifty dollars should be sufficient. Have about thirty-five dollars in various bills and the rest in change. You will find that you'll need a lot of change when you have many items in the twenty-five-to-fifty-cent range. Don't forget to *deduct* your float when you add up your cash receipts at the end of the day.

Make sure you have a sturdy cash box and that you *never, never* leave it unattended, or you might find yourself in a net loss position. It's sad to say, but there are people who cruise the garage sales whose idea of a bargain is an unattended cash box. If you have to go into the house to get something, *take the cash box with you.*

Generally, most items are paid for in cash. However, on a higher-priced item, it is not uncommon for a check to be offered as payment. If they don't have a good I.D. (that is, a drivers license *with a picture* or social security card), don't take it, no matter how good the price. Suggest that they leave a small cash deposit and you'll *hold* the item for them for a period of time until they can come back with the cash. In the meantime, if anyone else comes and wants the item, don't just say, "It's sold." Explain that somebody has put a deposit on it and if they will leave you their name and phone number you'll call them if the person who left the deposit forfeits.

Sometimes people will be interested in some of your "bigger ticket" items, but not at your price. Take their names and phone numbers and tell them you'll call them later if they don't sell for your price. You take the initiative — don't be shy. It's a garage sale — the purpose is to *sell* things.

Remember, planning ahead and common sense will make your one-shot mini-business a success. Look at Noah. While everyone else was liquidated, he was floating stock (Henny Youngmanicus, Greece, 55 A.D.).

CHAPTER 12

The Art of Haggling

Haggling is a lost art in most of North America. After all, when was the last time you walked into a major department store and haggled over the cost of a face towel? However, in many more civilized, passionate, earthy, and fun parts of the world, haggling is an integral part of the give-and-take of life. In some parts of the world, such as the Middle East, they would be positively insulted if you didn't bargain. In fact, they probably wouldn't know what to do with you since the only non-haggling persons they've ever encountered have been dead ones, and even then there have been some bones of contention.

Over here, in the wonderful western world where you say "sorry" if you accidentally touch someone on the bus — or slug them if they touch you — we consider haggling to be beneath us. Haggling is demeaning, a violation of our dignity, something that only gypsies and people who watch TV in their underwear do. Well, if you are going to have a garage sale, you'd better shift the old paradigm in the head a few degrees due east, because, like it or not, you are in the haggle biz.

You will find that once you get into it you'll rather enjoy it. Never be afraid to counter offer. If someone offers you five dollars for a radio you have marked for ten (and you're willing to take less) counter with seven-fifty. Who knows?

Watch out for the wily Bargooners. These are the folks who will come up to you with a bunch of items and offer you "five bucks for the lot." Before you say yes, add up the combined prices and see if it's a reasonable offer. Generally, we find the majority of such transactions are for a bunch of junk items, and intense haggling is out of the question for fear that they might actually change their minds and leave the junk. You will, of course, have to make some note in your bookkeeping that certain items sold as a "lot" so you can straighten out accounts later.

Remember, part of the reason for having the garage sale is to have a good time, so let down your hair and haggle. Try it, you'll like it.

★ ★ ★

"A penny saved is a penny Hearned."

Marvelous Marvin
Haggler

CHAPTER 13

The Big Day

Okay, the big day has arrived. You and your mate are all keyed up. The morning air feels charged with the prospects of free enterprise. You're like a prize race horse ready to show your stuff.

The Big Day

Your five-year-old is carrying your new Sony portable radio out to the sale table in the yard. You don't know this yet. Everything is go. Earlier in the week you've made the signs and stuck up the big ones announcing the event. (Do this at night. That way, you run less chance that anyone you know will see you on a ladder with a hammer in your hands and nails in your teeth looking like an idiot.) You've put up the direction signs. Make sure you stick up a good sign *in front of your house* and maybe some balloons or something else to attract attention. You'd be surprised how many people put up all sorts of signs and forget to mark their own house. A sandwich board on your car parked on the street is a good idea.

Another idea one of our readers suggested is to have a "free box." Put items in it that you just can't imagine anyone wanting. And let them go for FREE! This is the equivalent of a loss-leader in the retail trade — it gets people in, and, hopefully, they'll see something they want to buy. Part of the psychology here is guilt: If they get something for nothing they'll feel obligated to buy. (Make sure that you offer only one "freebie" per buyer.)

We've seen an interesting variation of this. It's a toy-box marked: "For kids under 10 — take one item FREE!" This is a little more insidious than the above. This works on getting the kids to work on their parents. Anyway, it works. But don't be surprised if you see your "free" items in somebody else's garage sale marked up for big bucks. Remember, one man's garbage is another man's inventory. Anyway, both these hints do work.

The garage has been swept out and the lawn tidied up.
You've managed to beg, borrow, or acquire enough tables
(you can use old doors on sawhorses — just cover them
with a sheet), and you're nearly ready to lay out the
goods. It's at this point you will probably run into the

dreaded Early Bird. The Early Bird is to garage sales what Godzilla is to Tokyo — a threat of total chaos and destruction. It is our candid opinion that these people are either illiterates or aliens as they seem incapable of reading simple signs such as: **No Early Birds, Please** . Of course, if they can read, they assume that you, of course, don't mean *them*.

They will try all sorts of excuses such as:

1. "I'm on my way to church and I won't be able to come back."

2. "We were just passing through the neighborhood and won't be coming back."

3. "We just want to look."

They will hound you, and if you give in to even *one* of them, the rest will descend upon you like a swarm of locusts.

Now we know you want a crowd, but not when you are trying to set things up. You don't need the aggravation of trying to go in and out of the house or direct everyone else where to put stuff with these people rummaging through the boxes *before you even get them out*. You will end up with some stuff sold, but nobody will have set up the cash table and made a record of it, and a whole bunch of disorganization will ensue that may take hours to sort out. So stick in there, and tell them to come back at the assigned opening hour.

No, they can't just look around! You need the space and time to set up properly. After all, stores don't let you in early. Be polite but firm. If you can't be polite then be rude and firm. After all, if you have advertised **No Early Birds** , what are they doing there anyway?

We have often requested that newspapers print our ads as **EARLY BIRDS WILL BE SHOT** ! However, they tend to frown on this.

There is, of course, an alternate method of handling Early Birds. This method stresses outfoxing them. You actually encourage them. You put on your signs or in your ads that Early Birds are welcome! If your ads state that the sale begins at 10:00 AM, you are actually ready to go at 9:00 AM. But be careful — this is the same type of person who lines up two days early for a Springsteen concert!

We suggest that you bring out a pot of coffee and some cookies or muffins. This serves two purposes. You have something to munch on when the sale is on if you can't get in the house, and it makes a "homey" atmosphere for browsing. If you're ambitious you can even sell coffee and muffins. We have been at street sales where they were selling hamburgers and hot dogs from a barbecue. We'd be careful before getting too far into food concessions because there are usually municipal health regulations covering the purveyance of bovine and carbonated edibles.

If you have a lot of clothing, try to rope off a small changing area with sheets. Watch for people who go in looking thin and come out fat.

Have paper and pens and pencils handy, as well as extra labels. This is for marking down prices or people's names and phone numbers who might want to leave a backup bid on some item. You might also want to jot down some numbers for personal reasons, which is quite understandable when you're making new friends at a garage sale.

You will find that the sale seems to go in spurts. There will be an initial rush of people, and then it will generally taper off until just after lunch. You will experience another rush of people until around three, then it will taper off again. Batteries of academics, sociologists, and demographers are working on heavily funded research grants to determine why this is so.

Around four you'll want to start to clean up. Gather all your signs as was mentioned in an earlier chapter, and put the remaining piles of goods into categories: stuff that is garbage, stuff for giving away to your local charity, and

Tip #18: IF YOU MUST GO INTO THE HOUSE, ALWAYS LEAVE SOMEONE TO LOOK AFTER THE CASH BOX.

stuff that you're saving for another garage sale.... and so on. With a little pitching in, this should take only an hour.

Then, finally, with the sun setting over the mortgaged rooftops and the odor of terminally barbecued beef wafting in from Gus Steinbrenner's laser-powered hibachi on the poolside of the fence, the moment you've been waiting for arrives: time to count up the loot.

After you've calculated the total *and deducted the float,* you can start to work out the accounts and see who sold the most, who made the most, and so on. If it is a neighborhood party we suggest some silly gifts (maybe from the junk that didn't sell) as "awards" for various categories.

Then you can take the money and buy more stuff that will eventually become inventory for next year's garage sale. In this way, the yearly cycle of human shopping mall migration and garage sale returns is kept intact, and the world and the seasons will continue to keep their appointed rounds. Isn't nature wonderful?

CHAPTER 14

What to Do with Leftovers

Hopefully, you won't have any, but just in case, if you're still stuck with some old familiar friends at the end of sale day, it's best to have a plan. Several options are available to you.

1. Set fire to the garage and be done with it. If you're bold enough, you might think about collecting on the insurance. (We don't recommend this.)

2. Call the Salvation Army and have them come and haul all or some of it away. What we generally do is call them well in advance so they come the next morning. That way, you get everything cleared away quickly and efficiently.

3. Put the stuff back in boxes and stash it away for your next garage sale.

4. Remember those people who said you inspired them to have their own garage sale? Well, pawn the stuff off on them to sell. This works for anyone who might have given you their stuff to sell and is now contemplating a garage sale. Mafiosi refer to it as "calling in favors."

5. Check for any names and phone numbers on any of the items that didn't sell. Maybe someone made a ridiculously low bid that now seems extremely generous.

6. Run an ad in the newspaper to sell any of the quality items you might not have sold.

7. Last but not least, throw it away or take it to the dump or, as a last resort, chop it finely with 1/4 cup parsley, 2 tsp. salt, and a good pinch of oregano and sauté over a medium flame for 15 minutes. Serves 4.

We think a combination of all the above (with the exception of #1) is usually the best idea.

APPENDIX 1

Timetable for Planning

One Month Before:

- Set the date.
- Involve the neighbors (optional).
- Define the area (i.e., carport, garage, yard).
- Start collecting stuff and:
    1. mark prices
    2. break up into categories
    3. store in marked boxes (i.e., "housewares").

Three Weeks Before:

- Decide the different table areas such as:
    1. electronics
    2. toys
    3. books
    4. household
    5. linens
    6. crafts
    7. books and records
    8. hardware and garden

Two Weeks Before:

- Start making signs.
- Get serious and go through entire house looking for junk. Check attic, crawl spaces, rafters . . . . you get the idea.
- Check deadlines for ads in papers.
- Arrange pickup of leftovers to coincide with the day after your sale.

One Week Before:

- Place ads.
- Set up plan for tables.
- Clean up all junk, wash clothing, etc.
- See if you have to rent anything, like tables, clothing racks, etc.
- Start collecting boxes, cardboard, and paper bags.

Three Days Before:

- Put up signs in laundromats, on billboards, etc.
- Put up signs on major thoroughfares.
- Make sure you have arrow signs ready.
- Get cash float.
- Draw up layout plan and make sure you have enough room.

Night Before:

- Put up remaining signs.
- Put up tables in the area.

APPENDIX 2

Making the Signs

Supplies:

- plenty of cardboard (old boxes are fine)
- felts or tempra paints
- large roll brown or white paper
- stapler
- staples
- pencils
- clear plastic wrap
- brushes if using paint
- paper clips
- if using stencil method, lightweight cardboard and craft knife
- time and patience

Method One:

1. Decide wording for pre-sale signs (include descriptive title to garage sale), direction signs (*remember which way arrows must point*), and categories of items to be sold.

2. Measure out paper to about three feet long.

3. Outline the letters by hand on brown or white paper (assign this to the neat and tidy members of the group).

4. When the first sign is all outlined, measure out several more pieces of paper approximately the same size and keep on lettering — the more you do the easier it gets. (Actually, your mind turns to mush and you lose all track of time.)

5. Color in lettering. Enlist everyone's aid for this, especially the kids. Also, use multi-colors to attract attention (felt or tempra paints are good).

6. Attach finished signs to cardboard pieces with staples. Cover with plastic wrap if there is any chance of rain.

7. Now, they're ready to be hung and do their job — advertise!

Method Two: (using a stencil)

1. Design your sign and draw on light cardboard. Make sure the sign is the size you want it to be in its finished form.

2. The lettering will be much easier to deal with if it is drawn in the block style because it will have to be cut out with a craft knife.

3. If no one in your group is comfortable with lettering skills, a store-bought stencil might be the answer.

4. After sign lettering has been drawn on light cardboard, cut each letter out using a craft knife.

5. Cut a piece of paper the size you have chosen for your signs.

6. Lay stencil on top of paper and anchor firmly using paper clips.

7. Paint over the cut-out letter to fill in the sign or use a pencil to stencil on the paper to be colored in later. You can also spray paint the signs this way.

8. As in Method One, attach to cardboard and cover with plastic wrap if necessary.

APPENDIX 3

Garage Layout

1. Draw scale layout of your sales area. The easiest way is to use graph paper.

2. Measure area in which you plan to hold your garage sale. In our example on the next page, the area is 12 x 25 feet.

3. Count the number of squares on the paper. In our example, the paper is 24 x 36 squares.

4. Divide the number of squares by the length and width. In our example, 24 divided by 12 and 36 divided by 25. Round off to the nearest whole number. In this case, the choice is 1 or 2. Choose the smaller scale (1 square equals 1 inch).

5. Measure your tables, bookcases, etc. Cut out cardboard sizes to scale so you will be able to shuffle them around easily to arrange your display areas. Remember to allow area between displays for moving around freely.

6. Have several final copies made so people unpacking your wares will know directly where they go and so you won't have to keep shuffling items back and forth and wasting time in setting up.

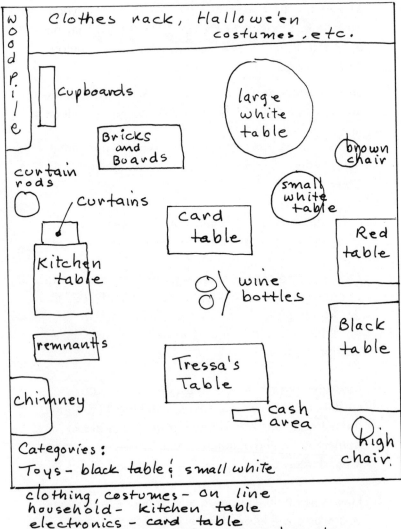

Wood Pile

Clothes rack, Hallowe'en costumes, etc.

Cupboards

large white table

Bricks and Boards

brown chair

curtain rods

small white table

curtains

card table

Red table

Kitchen table

wine bottles

remnants

Black table

Tressa's Table

chimney

cash area

high chair

Categories:
Toys — black table & small white
clothing, costumes — on line
household — kitchen table
electronics — card table
books, records — bricks and boards
patterns — kitchen table, remnants beside.

7. Assign table or display surface to each category.

8. If you're going to have a coffee pot set up, remember to plan its station near an outlet. (Hint: Have several outlets or an extension cord available — you may have electrical devices that people will want to test before they buy.)

9. The above garage layout planning can be particularly useful if you are holding a multi-family garage sale in a single shared space.

Sample Price Inventory

JONES GARAGE SALE

May 16-17

	asking price:	selling price:
HARDWARE AND GARDEN		
hack saw		
hammer		
curtain tracks		
old drill bits		
old files		
broken weed-eater		
push lawn mower		
HOUSEWARES		
pots		
vase		
spatulas, etc.		
cups (12)		
plates (9)		
old clock		
mantle radio		

	asking price:	selling price:

RECORDS

    Bobby Vinton
    Buddy Holly
    Electric Prunes
    The Kingsmen
    Chopin
    various 8-tracks (23)
    the complete Disco tapes

BOOKS

    paperback books (74)
    hardcover books (14)

ELECTRONICS

    old B & W TV
    Texas Instrument computer
    computer tapes
    burglar alarm
    house wiring fixtures (25)

TOYS

    roller skates
    crib toys (3)
    Care Bear
    Cabbage Patch Doll
    Barbie Doll
    HO electric train
    Master of the Universe
    jigsaw puzzles (4)

	asking price:	selling price:

CLOTHES

 children's snow suits (2)
 Halloween costumes (4)
 dresses (girls) (5)
 ties (12)
 dresses (ladies) (4)

CRAFTS

 doll clothes (7)
 candles (6)
 wind chimes (3)

TOTAL: